An Apple a Day

Folk Proverbs and Riddles

North American Folklore for Youth

An Apple a Day

Folk Proverbs
and Riddles

Gus Snedeker

Mason Crest

Mason Crest
370 Reed Road
Broomall, Pennsylvania 19008
www.masoncrest.com

Printed and bound in the United States of America.

First printing
9 8 7 6 5 4 3 2 1

Library of Congress Cataloging-in-Publication Data

Snedeker, Gus.
 An apple a day : folk proverbs and riddles / Gus Snedeker.
    p. cm.
  ISBN 978-1-4222-2493-9 (hardcover) — ISBN 978-1-4222-2486-1
(hardcover series) — ISBN 978-1-4222-9258-7 (ebook)
  1. Riddles, Juvenile. 2. Proverbs—Juvenile literature. I. Title.
 PN6371.5.S64 2012
 398.9—dc23
                                    2012011852

Produced by Harding House Publishing Services, Inc.
www.hardinghousepages.com
Cover design by Torque Advertising + Design.

Contents

✳ Introduction

by Dr. Alan Jabbour

What do a story, a joke, a fiddle tune, a quilt, a dance, a game of jacks, a holiday celebration, and a Halloween costume have in common? Not much, at first glance. But they're all part of the stuff we call "folklore."

The word "folklore" means the ways of thinking and acting that are learned and passed along by ordinary people. Folklore goes from grandparents to parents to children—and on to *their* children. It may be passed along in words, like the urban legend we hear from friends who promise us that it *really* happened to someone they know. Or it may be tunes or dance steps we pick up on the block where we live. It could be the quilt our aunt made. Much of the time we learn folklore without even knowing where or how we learned it.

Folklore is not something that's far away or long ago. It's something we use and enjoy every day! It is often ordinary—

and yet at the same time, it makes life seem very special. Folklore is the culture we share with others in our homes, our neighborhoods, and our places of worship. It helps tell us who we are.

Our first sense of who we are comes from our families. Family folklore—like eating certain meals together or prayers or songs—gives us a sense of belonging. But as we grow older we learn to belong to other groups as well. Maybe your family is Irish. Or maybe you live in a Hispanic neighborhood in New York City. Or you might live in the country in the middle of Iowa. Maybe you're a Catholic—or a Muslim—or you're Jewish. Each one of these groups to which you belong will have it's own folklore. A certain dance step may be African American. A story may have come from Germany. A hymn may be Protestant. A recipe may have been handed down by your Italian grandmother. All this folklore helps the people who belong to a certain group feel connected to each other.

Folklore can make each group special, different from all the others. But at the same time folklore is one of the best ways we can get to know to each other. We can learn about Vietnamese immigrants by eating Vietnamese foods. We can understand newcomers from Somalia by enjoying their music and dance. Stories, songs, and artwork move from group to group. And everyone is the richer!

Folklore isn't something you usually learn in school. Somebody, somewhere, taught you that jump-rope rhyme you know—but you probably can't remember *who* taught you. You definitely didn't learn it in a schoolbook, though! You can study folklore and learn about it—that's what you are doing now in this book!—but folklore normally is something that just gets passed along from person to person.

This series of books explores the many kinds folklore you can find across the North American continent. As you read, you'll learn something about yourself—and you'll learn about your neighbors as well!

✳ ONE
What Are Proverbs and Riddles?

Janie could not wait for her big brother to get home. He was coming home from college for the summer. He had called the night before to say he would get home around 2:00 in the afternoon. It was 9:00 in the morning now and Janie was already staring out the front window, waiting. Her dad came up and said, "I know you are very excited to see Chris again, but remember, a watched pot never boils!"

Janie turned and looked at her dad. "What does that mean, Dad?"

"Chris will be here at 2:00 no matter what you do. If you sit here the whole time, it will seem like he takes forever to get home. If you go outside and play with your friends, he will be here before you know it. Time flies when you are having fun!"

Janie was not sure exactly what her dad meant. She did go to play with her friends.

In the middle of a game of tag just a little while later, her mom called out, "Your brother is home!" Janie was amazed. Her dad was right. The time had gone by so fast. She ran in to greet her brother.

What Is a Proverb?

Proverbs and riddles are part of the oral tradition of America. Oral tradition is history that is only spoken. It is not written down. Oral tradition is told from person to person in stories, poems, songs—and proverbs and riddles. A culture's oral tradition is an important way that knowledge is passed down through generations.

A watched pot never boils.

Time flies when you are having fun.

Janie's dad uses these two common proverbs. What is a proverb? They are short phrases that tell a belief or a bit of wisdom. Proverbs give a lot of meaning in just a few words. These phrases are told from person to person through generations. They do not change much over time. A lot of the

---

DID YOU KNOW?

Proverbs are found in every language and culture.

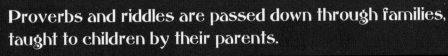

Proverbs and riddles are passed down through families, taught to children by their parents.

proverbs you hear today are most likely the same ones your great-grandparents heard when they were kids.

Proverbs can be either metaphorical or literal. A metaphorical proverb uses words that mean one thing to say something else. A literal proverb means exactly what it says. Here's an example:

Don't put all your eggs in one basket.

What does this mean? It could mean exactly what it says. Eggs can break. A lot of eggs in one basket could all break at once. You would be smart to put your eggs in a few baskets. That way if you dropped one basket you would still have other baskets with eggs in them. That is the literal meaning.

But the proverb is not really talking about "eggs" and "baskets." The eggs stand for something else, like money. The baskets stand for risk. For example you might spend all your allowance on one big toy or on five small toys. The one big toy might break, leaving you with nothing. If one little toy breaks, you still have four toys left. You did not put all your eggs (allowance) into one basket (toy). This is the metaphorical meaning of the proverb.

Here is another proverb:

Do not put off until tomorrow what you can do today.

What do you think? Is this proverb metaphorical or literal? Does it mean exactly what it says? Or do its words stand for another meaning?

Here's another one:

People who live in glass houses should not throw stones.

Can you tell whether this is metaphorical or literal?

Here are some more examples of metaphorical proverbs:

A bird in the hand is worth two in the bush.

A friend in need is a friend indeed.

If it ain't broke, don't fix it.

Monkey see, monkey do.

Don't put all your eggs in one basket.

Easy come, easy go.

Too many cooks spoil the soup.

Never put off until tomorrow what you can do today.

You can lead a horse to water, but you can't make him drink.

Where there's smoke, there's fire.

Bad weeds grow fast.

You can't have your cake and eat it too.

Red sky at night, sailor's delight.

Lightning never strikes twice in the same place.

Still waters run deep.

What do they think these proverbs mean?

What Is a Riddle?

Proverbs give you a bit of knowledge in a short phrase—but riddles test your knowledge. Riddles come in many forms. A riddle may be a short question, or a poem with a question at the end. Sometimes a riddle is just a statement with a puzzle hidden in the words. Riddles may be jokes or conundrums. A conundrum plays with words to confuse the listener. For example:

What is black and white and red all over?

If you heard this riddle instead of read it, you would not know whether "red" was spelled r-e-d or r-e-a-d. You would most likely guess that it meant the color red since black and white are colors also. The trick of this riddle is that the question is really, "What is black and white and READ all over?" The answer is, of course, a newspaper. This is probably one of the most well-known riddles in America!

Joke riddles test your smarts, but they are also funny. "Why did the chicken cross the road?" is one of the most famous joke riddles. The answer is so easy it is silly. The chicken crossed the road to get to the other side!

Throughout history, riddles have been used for more than just fun. Sometimes riddle contests were used instead of fights

> **DID YOU KNOW?**
> In J.R.R. Tolkien's *The Hobbit*, Bilbo Baggins and Gollum have a battle with riddles. Who wins? Read the book to find out!

with swords. Even if you never have to fight someone with riddles, it is good to know and understand them. Riddles—and proverbs—tell us a lot about our culture and our history.

What is black and white and red (read) all over?

Many proverbs have religious origins.

✳ TWO
Where Do Proverbs Come From?

Words to Understand

An *almanac* is a booklet put out once a year that has information about the stars and the weather, as well as other information.

A *playwright* is someone who writes plays.

Proverbs are used so often that we do not think about who first said them. So where did they come from? Proverbs come from many places. They come from books, religions, speeches, ideas about health—maybe even from advertising.

Religious

All the religions of the world have their own proverbs. Religions use proverbs to teach lessons important to the religion's beliefs. Some religious proverbs are ancient folk sayings that are used by the religion. Others are created to teach the religion's beliefs. Religious books like the Bible, the Koran, and others contain ancient proverbs that have been saved for thousands of years. Other religions pass proverbs down by word-of-mouth. Native American religions, for example, have no written texts. Many of their ancient proverbs might have been lost forever if they had not been written down.

RELIGIONS AND THEIR BOOKS

Buddhism: The Tripitaka

Christianity: The Bible

Confucianism: The Analects

Hinduism: The Bhagavad-Gita

Islam: The Koran

Judaism: The Torah

There are many proverbs in the Bible. There is even a whole section in the Hebrew Bible called the Book of Proverbs. Some proverbs from the Bible include, "You reap what you sow," and "For wisdom is better than rubies." What do you think these proverbs mean?

The Christian New Testament is also a source of proverbs. Jesus told stories called parables to teach lessons. Some of these stories have since been shortened into proverbs. One story Jesus told was about a woman who had been bad. Her neighbors were very upset with her. Some even wanted to throw stones at her. Jesus tells the crowd that the person who has never done anything wrong should throw the first stone. Of course, no one can claim to be perfect. No one throws a rock, and the crowd leaves the woman alone. This story is now known in the proverb, "Let anyone is perfect cast the first stone." It means you should not pick on someone else when you also have faults.

Confucianism is also a source of many well-known Chinese proverbs. Confucius was a wise man who lived around 500 BCE in China. The Chinese religion Confucianism is based on his sayings and teachings. Confucius's sayings are gathered into a book called The Analects of Confucius. Analects are sort of like proverbs. Some of the proverbs from Confucius are now well known even in North America. Here are a couple of his famous sayings.

Wisdom is recognizing what you know and what you don't.

Wherever you go, go with all your heart.

THE GOLDEN RULE

Confucius said, "What you do not wish for yourself, do not do to others." This is a version of the Golden Rule. The Golden Rule is a proverb that sets a basic rule for how to behave. There are versions of the Golden Rule in almost every major religion. Christianity's version is: "Do unto others as you would have them do unto you." All the different versions say the same thing: *Treat others how you want to be treated.*

Nonreligious Sources

Books or teachings that are not religious are called secular. There are many secular sources for proverbs. *Poor Richard's Almanac* by Benjamin Franklin is a well-known nonreligious source of proverbs. Franklin was an important person during the beginning of the United States. He was a signer of the Declaration of Independence. He was also a famous inventor. Ben Franklin published his proverbs in his **almanac**. Some of them he wrote himself. Other proverbs had been said for a long time before he printed them. Publishing the proverbs made them more popular. It also saved the proverbs for future generations.

Benjamin Franklin

BENJAMIN FRANKLIN

Benjamin Franklin was born in 1709 in Massachusetts. He only went to school for two years, but he never stopped learning. He was an inventor, a printer, and a scientist. He also spoke six languages!

Literature and poetry are also sources for proverbs. The famous *playwright* William Shakespeare is known for adding many new words to the English language. He also used many phrases in his plays that we know today as proverbs. For example, "A rose by any other name would smell as sweet" is from *Romeo and Juliet*. The proverb means that a name is not what makes you who you are.

ROMEO AND JULIET: A SUMMARY

Romeo and Juliet is one of the most famous sad love stories.

Romeo and Juliet are teenagers whose families do not like each other. Romeo and Juliet fall in love. They get married in secret. Romeo kills Juliet's cousin by accident. He has to leave town. Juliet's parents try to make her marry another man. Juliet fakes her own death to get out of the wedding. Romeo finds out she is dead and drinks poison to kill himself. Juliet kills herself after seeing Romeo dead by her side. The deaths of Romeo and Juliet help their families learn to get along.

Painting of Romeo and Juliet by Francesco Hayez.

Proverbs and Advertising

Melts in your mouth, but not in your hands.

Like a good neighbor, State Farm is there.

Do you know these phrases? They are two well-known advertising slogans. These slogans are not real proverbs. They are like proverbs because they are short phrases that give information. Companies make up these slogans that sound sort of like proverbs to sell their products. Many advertising slogans are so well known they are almost like modern proverbs. The Nike slogan, "Just do it" might be one example. Can you think of some others? There are also proverbs that have to do with buying or selling things that are not slogans. "The customer is always right" and "You break it, you buy it" are two examples.

Healthy Proverbs

Many proverbs deal with health and medicine. We all know that an apple a day keeps the doctor away, and that laughter is the best medicine, right? These are both proverbs. Eating an apple each day does not really keep you from having to see the doctor. But fruit is an important part of a healthy diet. A healthy diet helps keep your body strong. A strong body can fight off sickness. So, in a way, an apple a day does help keep the doctor

NEW PROVERBS

Even the oldest proverbs were new once. Who first said
them? Sometimes we don't know. But new ones are
being spoken all the time. They come from politicians.
They come from music. They may come from movies or
television shows. Do you recognize these modern sayings?
Do you think they are proverbs now?

*Ask not what your country can do for you; ask what you can do
for your country.*
  –President John F. Kennedy

If you can't take the heat, get out of the kitchen.
  –President Harry S. Truman

All you need is love.
  –The Beatles ("All You Need Is Love")

away! And scientists have found that laughing actually is good
for your body. It helps your body fight infection.

Health proverbs give advice about how to stay well. After
all, if you never get sick, you never need a cure. As the proverb

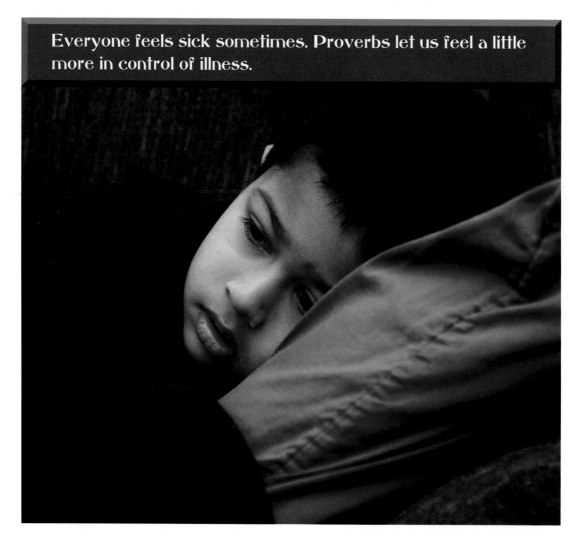

Everyone feels sick sometimes. Proverbs let us feel a little more in control of illness.

says, "An ounce of prevention is worth a pound of cure." In other words, spend a little extra time keeping yourself healthy. If you do this, you will not have to spend a lot of time curing yourself later.

Most health proverbs are old. They were first said a long time ago when there were not many doctors. Or the doctors were not very good. It truly was safer to just not get sick. Do these proverbs still make sense to you now? Doctors and hospitals are much better. Is it still better to do things to keep yourself from getting sick? Is health still better than wealth?

OTHER HEALTHY PROVERBS

Feed a cold, starve a fever.
   (In other words, you should eat when you have a cold, but not eat if you have a fever.)

Early to bed, early to rise, makes you healthy, wealthy, and wise.
   (Get enough sleep if you want to be healthy, successful, and smart!)

Eat to live, not live to eat.
   (Eat just enough to keep your body healthy, rather than spending your whole life thinking about eating.)

Moderation in all things.
   (Too much of anything can be unhealthy.)

Children and teenagers today live in a different world than their parents and grandparents did—but they still sometimes say the same proverbs.

✳ THREE
What Does That Proverb Mean?

Words to Understand

Prejudice is when you have a bad opinion of someone without even knowing that person. Prejudice is often based on what someone looks like or what group someone belongs to.

Everyday life now is a lot different from what it was two hundred years ago. A lot has changed in the world. Today we think things like video games and cell phones are normal. Two hundred years ago these everyday things would have seemed like magic. A kid would not know words like e-mail and website. In the same way, things and words from two hundred years ago might be weird to you.

This happens with proverbs also. Sometimes proverbs are so old that they do not make sense to people today. The original meaning is lost. Sometimes the proverb refers to something that no longer exists. Other times a proverb may carry *prejudice* from the past.

One proverb that might not make sense to someone today is, "Good fences make good neighbors." What do you think it means? It sounds like it means that having a fence around your house is a good way to keep yourself away from other people. The real meaning is that fences help neighbors respect each other. New England farmers used to build stone fences to mark the edge of their land. These farmers made up the proverb to say that it is important to respect your neighbor's space. It could even mean that it is good to be respectful of other people in general. Other proverbs that value respect include, "Live and let live," and "One man's trash is another man's treasure."

A good fence makes a good neighbor!

How about this proverb: "Little pitchers have big ears?" Have you ever heard a grownup say that when she wanted to point out that children were listening to the conversation? You may understand what the proverb means—"Be careful what you say because children may be listening"—without understanding where the proverb's meaning came from in the first place. It's a metaphorical proverb that uses the handles ("the big ears") on a milk pitcher to make a point about kids who may sit quietly listening while grownups talk.

Proverbs from other countries or cultures might also be hard to understand. Read these proverbs from around the world. Do they make sense to you? What do you think they mean? What are their metaphorical meanings?

The worse the passage the more welcome the port.
　　—English proverb

In a court of birds, the cockroach never wins his case.
　　—Rwandan proverb

Don't think there are no crocodiles because the water is calm.
　　—Malayan proverb

In a battle between elephants, the ants get squashed.
　　—Thai proverb

Children growing up in different cultures will learn different proverbs. And their parents will tell different proverbs about child-raising.

Bad Proverbs

Some old proverbs carry meanings that no longer match modern beliefs. Many of these have to do with racist ideas or stereotypes. For example, we no longer think, "a woman's place is in the home," or, "the only good Indian is a dead Indian." These are both old sayings that we know are not true. They are based on old ways of thinking. These proverbs teach us about some of the negative history of our country. Learning about history can help us understand some current problems. History can also teach us how not to act. In fact, there is a proverb

HOW TO RAISE CHILDREN

Every culture has different ideas about how to raise children. These two proverbs give two different ideas about how to show children the right way to act.

The burnt child dreads the fire.
   (This proverb is saying that painful punishment is the best way to teach children how to act.)

Tell me and I'll forget. Show me, and I may not remember. Involve me, and I'll understand.
   (This Native American proverb says that children learn by doing.)

about this: "Those who fail to learn from history are doomed to repeat it."

Sadly, some racist ideas and feelings are still around today. When you hear a proverb, listen for any words that might be racist. Think before you speak—will the proverb hurt someone's feelings? If so, don't say it. Even if all your friends are saying it, think for yourself. Remember, "If everyone else jumped off a bridge, would you?"

When Oedipus finds out the truth about his mother, he is so upset he puts out his own eyes and becomes blind.

✳ FOUR
Riddles and Wisdom

Have you heard the sad story of Oedipus?

Oedipus is the Prince of Thebes. When Oedipus is born a fortune-teller says that when he grows up he will kill his father and marry his mother. The king does not want this to happen so he sends Oedipus away with a servant to be killed. The servant cannot kill the cute little baby. The servant leaves Oedipus in the wild.

Oedipus is adopted and raised far away from Thebes. He is happy until a fortune-teller tells him his fate is to kill his father and marry his mother. Oedipus loves his parents, so he leaves home to keep them safe.

While traveling, Oedipus fights and kills the King of Thebes (his real father). Then, he arrives at Thebes to find the city blocked by a scary creature called the Sphinx. The Sphinx makes Oedipus answer a riddle in order to get into the city.

"What animal walks on four feet in the morning, two feet at noon, and three feet in the evening?"

Oedipus figures out the answer.

"A human crawls on hands and knees when a baby, walks on two legs when an adult, and uses a cane when old."

The Sphinx dies from shock when Oedipus solves the riddle. The city of Thebes is safe again. As a reward, Oedipus becomes king and marries the queen (his real mother).

Learning from Riddles

The story of Oedipus has a riddle in it, but the story is kind of a riddle itself. If no one had listened to the fortune-teller, would his vision have come true? The story of Oedipus uses riddles to teach an important lesson. You are in charge of your own fate.

Riddles test our knowledge and wisdom. Riddles are used in books and stories to show that knowledge is more important than strength or beauty. Socrates, an ancient Greek philosopher, used riddles to teach about the meaning of life. His riddles often had no answers. Socrates used his riddles to keep people thinking about the most important things in life. Socrates died a long time ago. His riddles are still around today. You might learn about Socrates in school, and you might even hear some of his riddles.

Riddles in School

Sometimes school is not fun. Riddles, and puzzles can be used to make learning more interesting. Most people think it is fun to solve riddles. All problems can be viewed in the same way. Take

TEST YOUR KNOWLEDGE
WITH THESE ANCIENT RIDDLES

"At night, they come without being fetched,

And by day they are lost without being stolen."

   Hint: They light up the night.

"The beginning of eternity

The end of time and space

The beginning of every end

And the end of every place."

   Hint: It is used fourteen times in this riddle.

"There was a green house.

Inside the green house there was a white house.

Inside the white house there was a red house.

Inside the red house there were lots of babies."

   Hint: A summertime fruit.

(Answers: the stars; the letter "e"; a watermelon)

Photo of some of the villians from *Batman*. From left: The Penguin (Burgess Meredith), The Riddler (Frank Gorshin), and The Joker (Cesar Romero).

DID YOU KNOW?
Batman's enemy, "The Riddler" give clues about his crimes using riddles and puzzles.

---

math class, for example. A lot of kids do not enjoy math. But, word problems in math are like riddles. Can you solve this one?

School starts at 8:00 am. Greg takes 10 minutes to shower, and 4 minutes to brush his teeth. Greg spends 16 minutes getting dressed, eating his breakfast, and packing his bag. His ride to school takes another 15 minutes. What time does Greg have to wake up to be on time for school?

(Answer: 7:15)

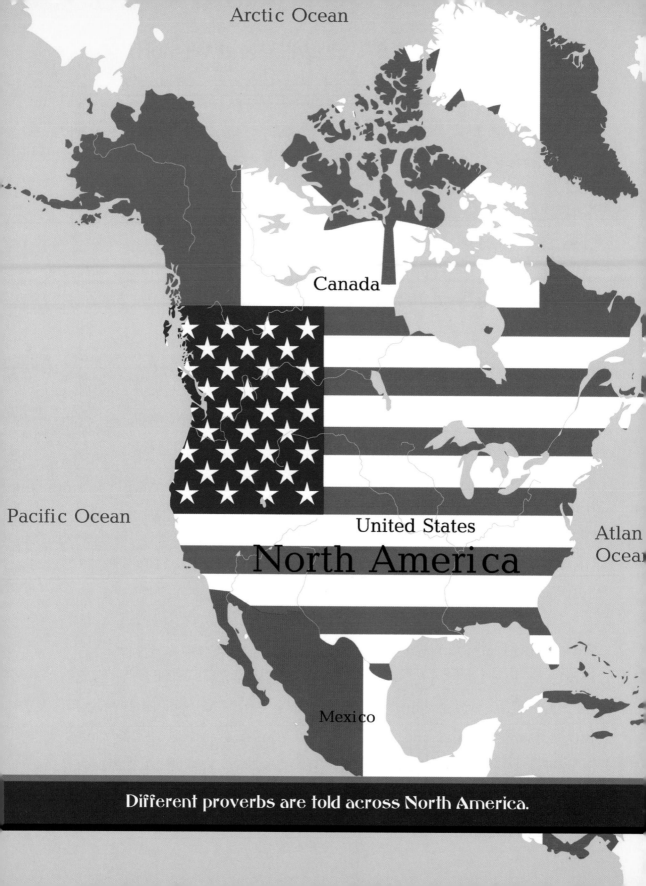

Arctic Ocean

Canada

Pacific Ocean

United States

North America

Atlan
Ocean

Mexico

Different proverbs are told across North America.

✳ FIVE
Proverbs and Riddles of North America

When you hear the word, "America," you probably think of the United States. But, North America is a continent that also includes the countries of Canada and Mexico. Ideas have been shared between all three countries for hundreds of years. Now ideas are shared around the world because of globalization. The Internet and other technology let information travel easily from place to place. As ideas travel and cultures mix, it gets harder to see where an idea or tradition originally started.

The proverbs and riddles we know in North America are not just American, Canadian, or Mexican. People come from all over the world to live in North America. These immigrants brought their beliefs, food, and traditions with them. They also brought their proverbs and riddles. Also, different regions in North America have created traditions and ideas, including new proverbs and riddles.

American Proverbs

"You have to kiss a lot of toads before you find a handsome prince."

"You cannot unscramble eggs."

Canadian Proverb

"Save your breath to cool your porridge."

Mexican Proverbs

"It is not enough to know how to ride, you must also know how to fall."

Let no one say, "Of this water I won't drink," no matter how muddy it looks, it may quench your thirst."

Native American Proverbs

"Do not judge a man until you have walked two moons in his moccasins." (Cheyenne)

"The more you give, the more good things come to you." (Crow)

"God gives each a song." (Ute)

Regional Riddles

Riddles are usually not passed from generation to generation in the same way as proverbs. This is because riddles are often thought of on the spot to test someone's knowledge. Here are some Canadian riddles:

> "How do you make anti-freeze?
> *You put ice in her bed!*

> What do you get when you cross a bear and a skunk?
> *Winnie the Pee-u!*

Is there anything about these riddles that makes them seem "Canadian?" Do the jokes or riddles you know fit with your region or cultural heritage?

Proverbs and riddles are important parts of folk traditions around the world. They give information and test our knowledge. Old proverbs still have meaning in our modern world. Some proverbs tell us the right or wrong way to act. Riddles may make us laugh, but they also test our brains. Proverbs and riddles make us think!

Find Out More

In Books

Bierhorst, John, editor. *Lightening Inside You: And Other Native American Riddles*. New York: William Morrow, 2002.

Cousineau, Phil and Wes Scoop Nisker. *A World Treasury of Riddles*. Berkeley, Calif.: Conari, 2001.

Stewart, Julia. *African Proverbs and Wisdom: A Collection for Every Day of the Year, from More than Forty African Nations.* New York: Kensington, 2002.

Swann, Brian. *Touching the Distance: Native American Riddle-Poems.* San Diego, Calif.: Browndeer Press, 2008.

On the Internet

Proverbs

www.afriprov.org

www.oneliners-and-proverbs.com

Riddles

www.fun4children.com

www.justriddlesandmore.com

www.niehs.nih.gov/kids/braint/htm

Index

Picture Credits

About the Author and the Consultant

Gus Snedeker is proud of his heritage as a Dutch American. He loves to study the stories and traditions of the various groups of people who helped build America. He has also written several other books in this series.

Dr. Alan Jabbour is a folklorist who served as the founding director of the American Folklife Center at the Library of Congress from 1976 to 1999. Previously, he began the grant-giving program in folk arts at the National Endowment for the Arts (1974-76). A native of Jacksonville, Florida, he was trained at the University of Miami (B.A.) and Duke University (M.A., Ph.D.). A violinist from childhood on, he documented old-time fiddling in the Upper South in the 1960s and 1970s. A specialist in instrumental folk music, he is known as a fiddler himself, an art he acquired directly from elderly fiddlers in North Carolina, Virginia, and West Virginia. He has taught folklore and folk music at UCLA and the University of Maryland and has published widely in the field.